MW01630962

2024

www.13moonsdiary.com

BLOOD MOON

People are made of paper, love affairs,
    anything that tears easily.
A pregnant woman stands under the lunar eclipse,
    carves a swirl into a tree,
her baby is born with this same mark on his thigh.
It's just like the earth to come between the sun and the moon
    and cause this kind of mystery.
Point at a rainbow, and it will plummet and slice your finger off.
Use your lips instead, to show others what you are looking at.
Don't stand on high rocks or they will push you into the sky,
    and you will be pressed like a flower in a book.
People are made from rain showers, hatred, smears of spit,
    anything that might evaporate instantly.
That night, the moon was a true blood red,
not the pale rust of this moon, this morning.
    An entire human body coated red with blood,
    except where a path of tears washed through.
Don't stare at the moon
    or it will follow you persistently like a stray cat you have fed.
Don't hold out your hands when the sun is shining,
    or you will burn continually with possibility.
People are made of buckets of sand, sequins of clay, desire,
    anything that washes away easily.
Don't inhale too deeply, the scent of fallen leaves
pasted to the forest floor after a fresh rain,
    or you will be repeatedly stepped on.
Don't count the seeds in a mound of bear scat
    or just as many clouds will split open above your head.

Elizabeth Jacobson

Welcome to the 7th edition of 13 Moons Lunar Diary

If you were to ask me what I value most, what I consider the true measure of life, my answer is: Time Sovereignty. The freedom to decide what I do, when I do it, with whom and for whom - this is what I have come to hold dear. This is the essence of true privilege.
The exploitation of humans is too often connected to stealing access to our own time. Working 2 to 3 jobs just to make ends meet - on top of caring for family - this breeds not only exhaustion but steals the possibility of rest, connection to nature, friendships, community building - all of which nourish the human spirit. I want to live in world where we all have Time. Time to imagine what else is possible. Time to remember the deep truths that connect us to ourselves and each other. Time to create systems that value how we live rather than what we own.

TRUE WEALTH IS MEASURED IN TIME.
NOT MY TIME AT THE EXPENSE OF YOURS - BUT MY TIME IN RELATIONSHIP WITH YOURS.

What is your relationship with Time?
What do you notice when you give yourself Time?
Who do you like to be and what Seasons spark your spirit?
Where are you drawn and what dreams come your way?

It is my hope that you engage this lunar diary
to explore your answers to these questions and yours.

This diary centers the ritual of tracking cycles of Time around the recurring node of the dark moon, inviting you to unearth, observe and document Time as you experience it, to notice the lunar shapes that animate the other rhythms of your life: dreams, moods, foods, blood, fertility, visions and venoms.

There are 13 LUNATIONS starting December 2023 and ending December 2024, each beginning with the New Moon and ending before the next. Within each lunar illustration you will find an inner circle and daily leaf that allows you to track any other cycle along with the lunar phases. Write or draw in the daily leaves. Color or number the circles. Write, draw, doodle as you wish!

A full page for each New Moon invites space for welcoming the darkness and setting intentions for the lunar cycle ahead. The daily pages that follow invite you to track and journal as you move towards the light of the Full Moon where you are given another full page for the expression of those intentions.

The illustration that bookends the diary offers a wider visual lens for the many cycles that influence our lives: Seasons, physical changes and developmental initiations can all be correlated to the lunar cycle.

Take your Time,
Meg Heather Ford

SUGGESTIONS FOR USE

This diary is intentionally designed to allow for numerous ways to track and document your time along side the phases of the moon. While there is no one way to use it, here are a few suggestions to consider:

- You may track your mood, food, dreams or daily experiences
- You may track your menstruation/ovulation cycle by coloring in the smaller circles to support either planning or avoiding conception
- If tracking your pregnancy, you may number the weeks along side the lunar phases
- If entering or exiting menopause, you may notice the new ways and rhythms to reorient your connection with the Moon

ECLIPSE

This edition includes a small graphic on the six New and Full Moon eclipses illustrating where on Earth they may be visible on that date.

A SOLAR ECLIPSE can only happen during a New Moon when the moon moves between the Earth and the Sun. There are between 2 and 5 solar eclipses every year and are either total, partial or annular, depending on how much of the sun is covered by the Moon.

Conversely, a LUNAR ECLIPSE can only happen with the Full Moon when the Earth comes directly between the Sun and Moon, preventing its rays from reaching the Moon. These are either total, partial or penumbral, depending on how much of the Earth's shadow covers the Moon's surface.

the seasonal illustration to the right
has been designed in color as a 11x14 wall poster,
available for purchase at www.13moonsdiary.com

WINTER

INFANT / CRONE
BIRTH / DEATH

NOURISH

YIN OF YIN

AUTUMN

MAGA
MENOPAUSE

GATHER

YANG TO YIN

YIN TO YANG

GROW

MAIDEN
MENARCHE

SPRING

YANG OF YANG

MOVE

BIRTH / CREATION
MOTHER

SUMMER

Visions for your year

December 12 2023 to January 10 2024

December

SU	MO	TU	WE	TH	FR	SA
					1	2
3	4	5	6	7	8	9
10	11	12	13	14	15	16
17	18	19	20	21	22	23
24	25	26	27	28	29	30
31						

January

SU	MO	TU	WE	TH	FR	SA
	1	2	3	4	5	6
7	8	9	10	11	12	13
14	15	16	17	18	19	20
21	22	23	24	25	26	27
28	29	30	31			

SEATTLE 15:32 TU DEC 12 NEW MOON

intention

NEW YORK 18:32 TU DEC 12

LONDON 23:32 TU DEC 12

HONG KONG 07:32 WE DEC 13

WE DEC 13 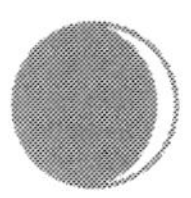

 TH DEC 14

FR DEC 15 

SA DEC 16

SU DEC 17

TU DEC 19 

 WE DEC 20

19:27 WINTER SOLSTICE

TH DEC 21

FR DEC 22 

SA DEC 23

SU DEC 24

expression

TH DEC 28

FR DEC 29

SA DEC 30

SU DEC 31

MO JAN 1

TU JAN 2

WE JAN 3

TH JAN 4

FR JAN 5

SA JAN 6

SU JAN 7

MO JAN 8

TU JAN 9

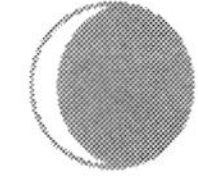

WE JAN 10

JANUARY 11 2024 TO FEBRUARY 8 2024

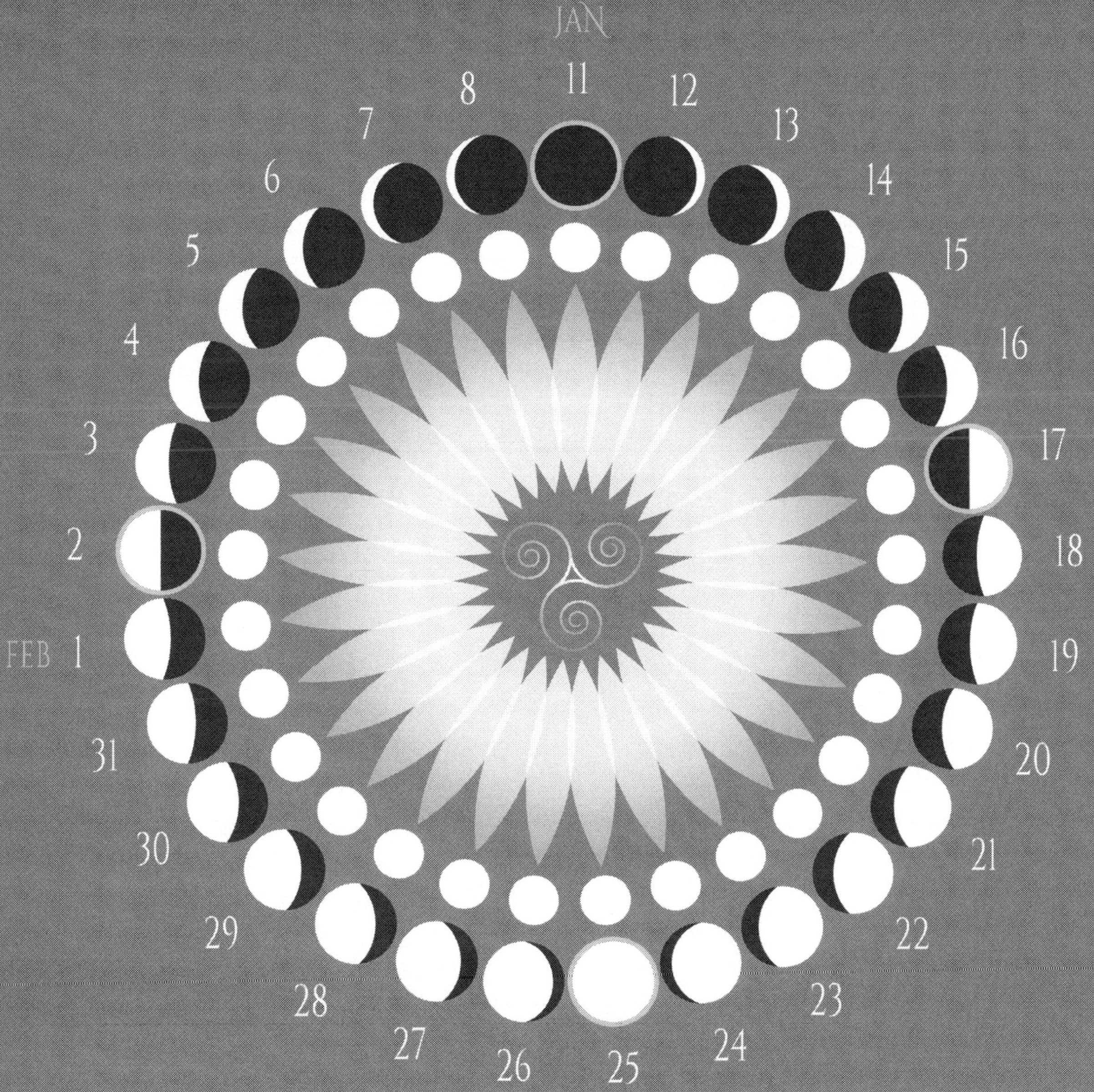

JANUARY

SU	MO	TU	WE	TH	FR	SA
	1	2	3	4	5	6
7	8	9	10	11	12	13
14	15	16	17	18	19	20
21	22	23	24	25	26	27
28	29	30	31			

FEBRUARY

SU	MO	TU	WE	TH	FR	SA
				1	2	3
4	5	6	7	8	9	10
11	12	13	14	15	16	17
18	19	20	21	22	23	24
25	26	27	28	29		

SEATTLE 03:57 TH JAN 11 NEW MOON

intention

NEW YORK 06:57
TH JAN 11

LONDON 11:57
TH JAN 11

HONG KONG 19:57
TH JAN 11

FR JAN 12 

SU JAN 14

MO JAN 15

TU JAN 16

WE JAN 17

TH JAN 18 

 FR JAN 19

SA JAN 20

SU JAN 21 

MO JAN 22

TU JAN 23

expression

SA JAN 27

SU JAN 28

MO JAN 29

TU JAN 30

WE JAN 31

TH FEB 1

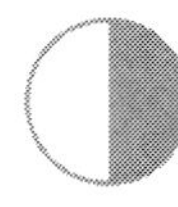
FR FEB 2

SA FEB 3

SU FEB 4

MO FEB 5

TU FEB 6

TH FEB 8

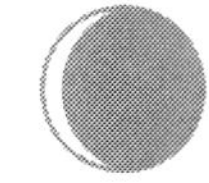

February 9 2024 to March 9 2024

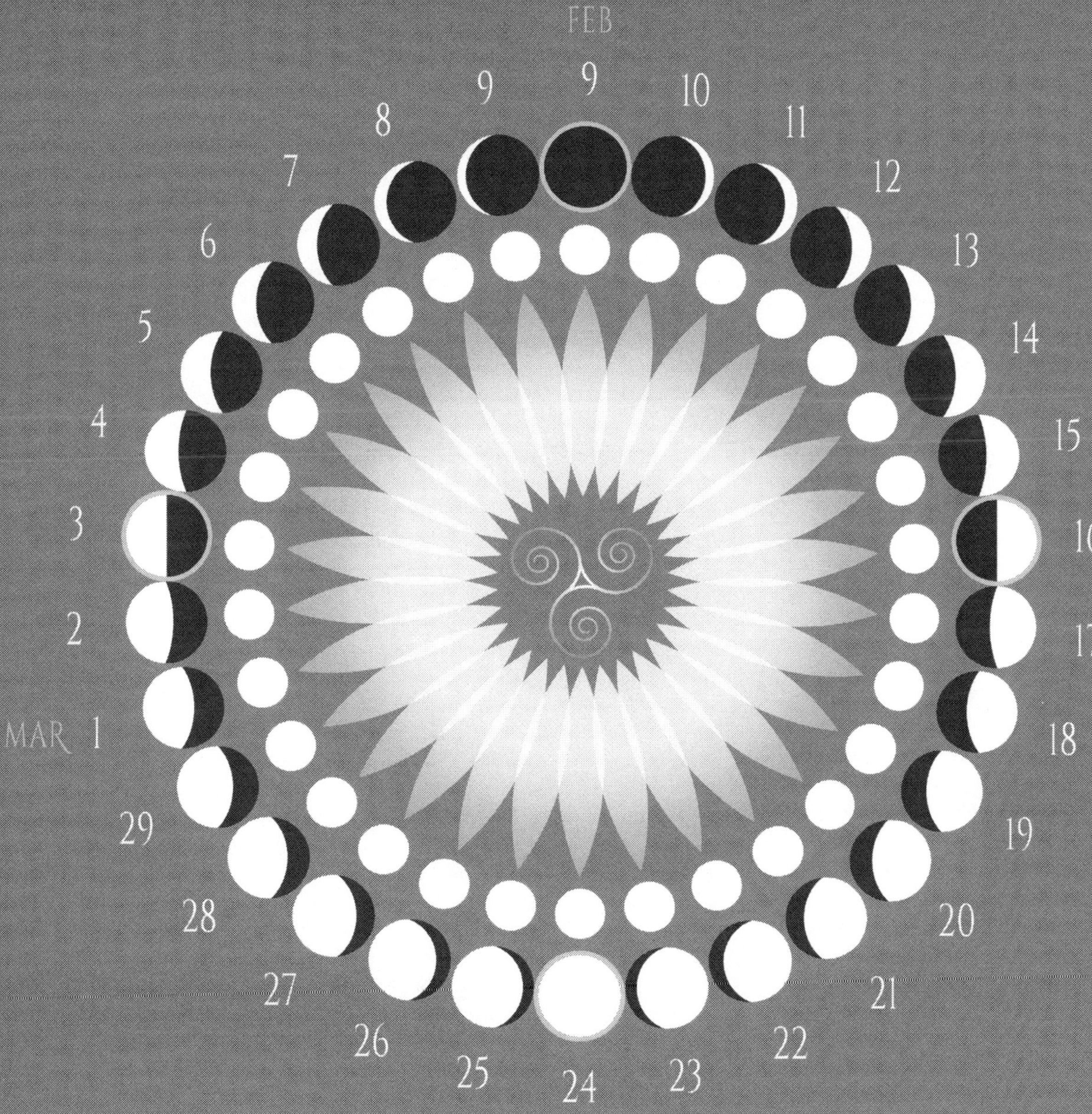

FEB

9 9 10 11 12 13 14 15 16 17 18 19 20 21 22 23 24 25 26 27 28 29

MAR 1 2 3 4 5 6 7 8 9

FEBRUARY

SU	MO	TU	WE	TH	FR	SA
				1	2	3
4	5	6	7	8	9	10
11	12	13	14	15	16	17
18	19	20	21	22	23	24
25	26	27	28	29		

MARCH

SU	MO	TU	WE	TH	FR	SA
					1	2
3	4	5	6	7	8	9
10	11	12	13	14	15	16
17	18	19	20	21	22	23
24	25	26	27	28	29	30
31						

SEATTLE 14:59 FR FEB 9 NEW MOON

intention

NEW YORK 17:59 LONDON 22:59 HONG KONG 06:59

FR FEB 9 FR FEB 9 SA FEB 10

SA FEB 10 

 SU FEB 11

MO FEB 12

TU FEB 13

WE FEB 14

TH FEB 15

FR FEB 16 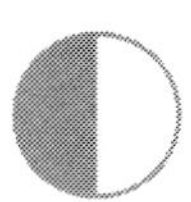

 SA FEB 17

SU FEB 18 

MO FEB 19 

 TU FEB 20

WE FEB 21

TH FEB 22 

FR FEB 23

expression

MO FEB 26 

TU FEB 27

WE FEB 28

TH FEB 29

FR MAR 1

SA MAR 2

SU MAR 3 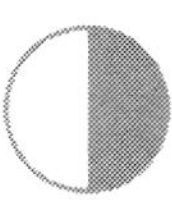

 MO MAR 4

TU MAR 5

WE MAR 6 

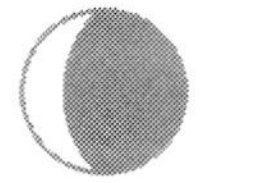

TH MAR 7

SA MAR 9

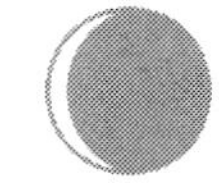

MARCH 10 2024 TO APRIL 7 2024

MARCH

SU	MO	TU	WE	TH	FR	SA
					1	2
3	4	5	6	7	8	9
10	11	12	13	14	15	16
17	18	19	20	21	22	23
24	25	26	27	28	29	30
31						

APRIL

SU	MO	TU	WE	TH	FR	SA
	1	2	3	4	5	6
7	8	9	10	11	12	13
14	15	16	17	18	19	20
21	22	23	24	25	26	27
28	29	30				

SEATTLE 01:00 SU MAR 10 NEW MOON

intention

NEW YORK 05:00
SU MAR 10

LONDON 09:00
SU MAR 10

HONG KONG 17:00
SU MAR 10

MO MAR 11

TU MAR 12

WE MAR 13

TH MAR 14 

 FR MAR 15

SA MAR 16

SU MAR 17 

MO MAR 18

SPRING EQUINOX 20:06

TU MAR 19 

WE MAR 20

FR MAR 22

SA MAR 23 

SU MAR 24

SEATTLE 00:00 MO MAR 25

expression

LUNAR ECLIPSE

PENUMBRAL MAR 24-25

○ NEW YORK 03:00
MO MAR 25

○ LONDON 07:00
MO MAR 25

○ HONG KONG 15:00
MO MAR 25

WE MAR 27

TH MAR 28

SA MAR 30

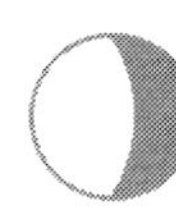

SU MAR 31

MO APR 1

TU APR 2 

WE APR 3

TH APR 4

FR APR 5

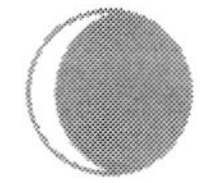
SA APR 6

APRIL 8 2024 TO MAY 6 2024

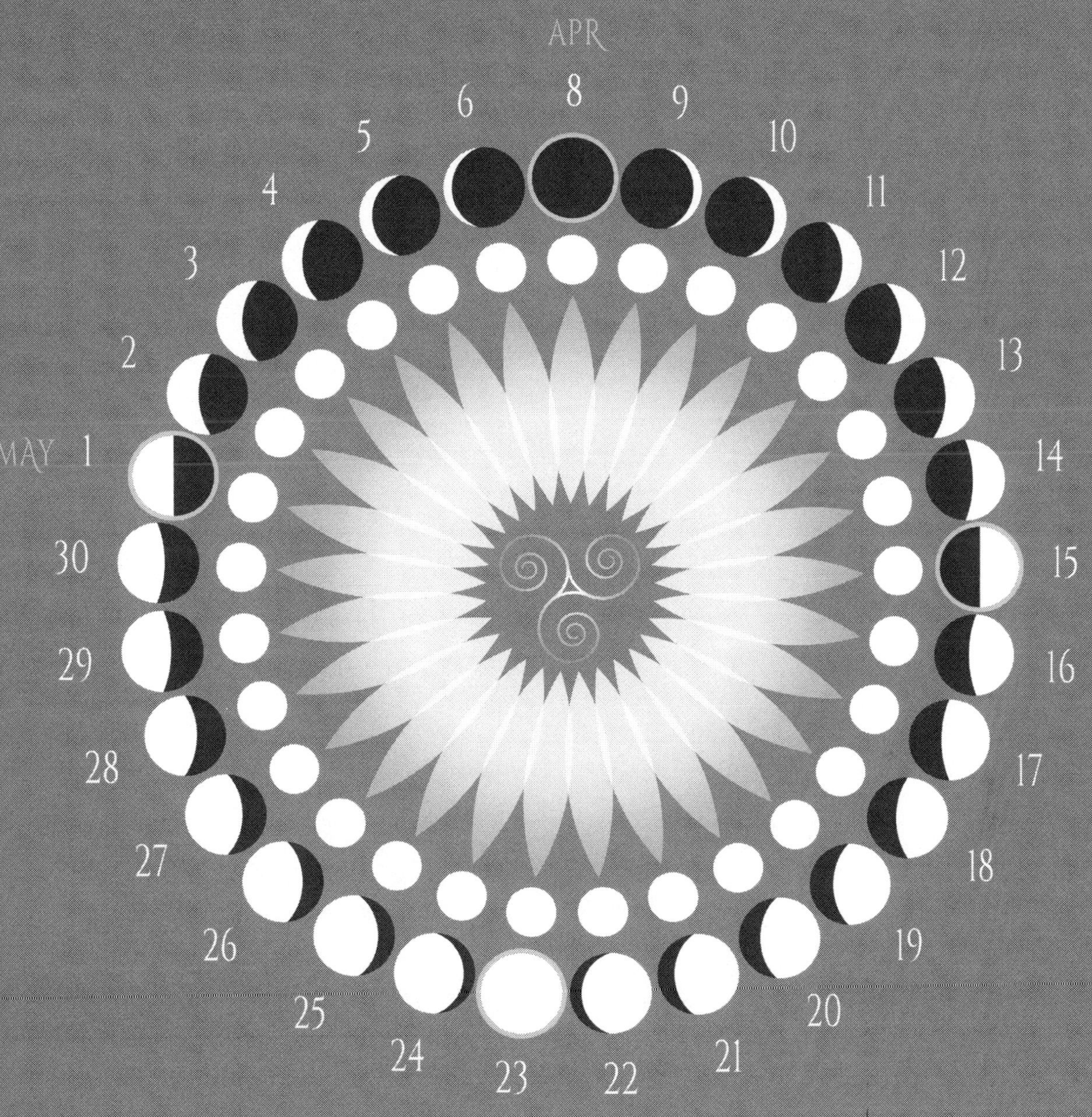

APRIL

SU	MO	TU	WE	TH	FR	SA
	1	2	3	4	5	6
7	8	9	10	11	12	13
14	15	16	17	18	19	20
21	22	23	24	25	26	27
28	29	30				

MAY

SU	MO	TU	WE	TH	FR	SA
			1	2	3	4
5	6	7	8	9	10	11
12	13	14	15	16	17	18
19	20	21	22	23	24	25
26	27	28	29	30	31	

SEATTLE 11:20 MO APR 8  NEW MOON

intention

SOLAR ECLIPSE

TOTAL APR 8

NEW YORK 14:20 MO APR 8

LONDON 19:20 MO APR 8

HONG KONG 02:20 TU APR 9

TU APR 9 

 WE APR 10

TH APR 11 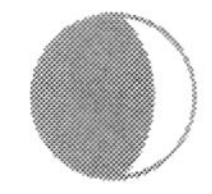

FR APR 12

SA APR 13

SU APR 14

MO APR 15

WE APR 17

TH APR 18 

 FR APR 19

SA APR 20

SU APR 21 

MO APR 22

SEATTLE 16:48 TU APR 23 FULL MOON

expression

NEW YORK 19:48 TU APR 23
LONDON 00:48 WE APR 24
HONG KONG 07:48 WE APR 24

TH APR 25

FR APR 26

SA APR 27

SU APR 28 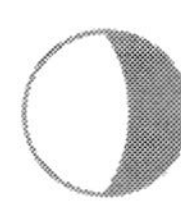

 MO APR 29

WE MAY 1

TH MAY 2

FR MAY 3

SA MAY 4

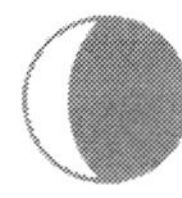

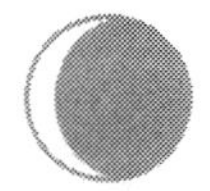

SU MAY 5

MO MAY 6

MAY 7 2024 TO JUNE 5 2024

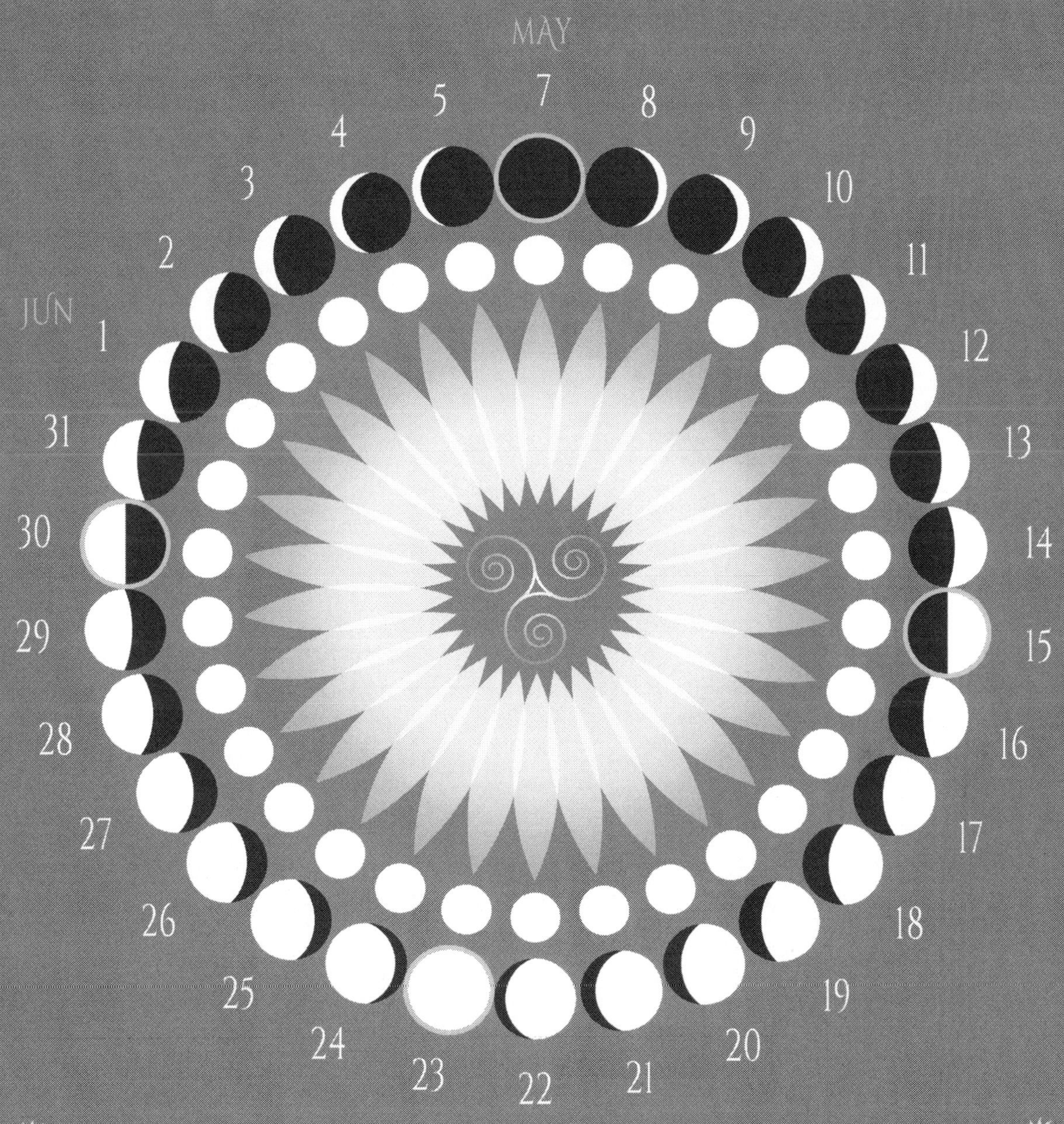

MAY

SU	MO	TU	WE	TH	FR	SA
			1	2	3	4
5	6	7	8	9	10	11
12	13	14	15	16	17	18
19	20	21	22	23	24	25
26	27	28	29	30	31	

JUNE

SU	MO	TU	WE	TH	FR	SA
						1
2	3	4	5	6	7	8
9	10	11	12	13	14	15
16	17	18	19	20	21	22
23	24	25	26	27	28	29
30						

SEATTLE 20:21 TU MAY 7 NEW MOON

intention

NEW YORK 23:21 TU MAY 7

LONDON 04:21 WE MAY 8

HONG KONG 11:21 WE MAY 8

WE MAY 8 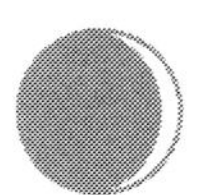

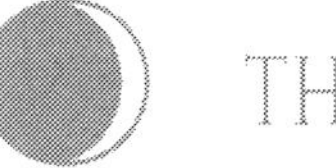 TH MAY 9

SA MAY 11

SU MAY 12

MO MAY 13

TU MAY 14

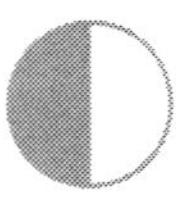

WE MAY 15

TH MAY 16

FR MAY 17

SA MAY 18

SU MAY 19

MO MAY 20 

TU MAY 21

WE MAY 22

expression

FR MAY 24

SA MAY 25

SU MAY 26

MO MAY 27

TU MAY 28 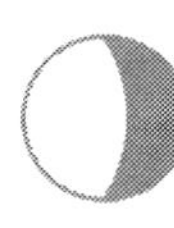

 WE MAY 29

FR MAY 31 

SA JUN 1

SU JUN 2

MO JUN 3

TU JUN 4

JUNE 6 2024 TO JULY 4 2024

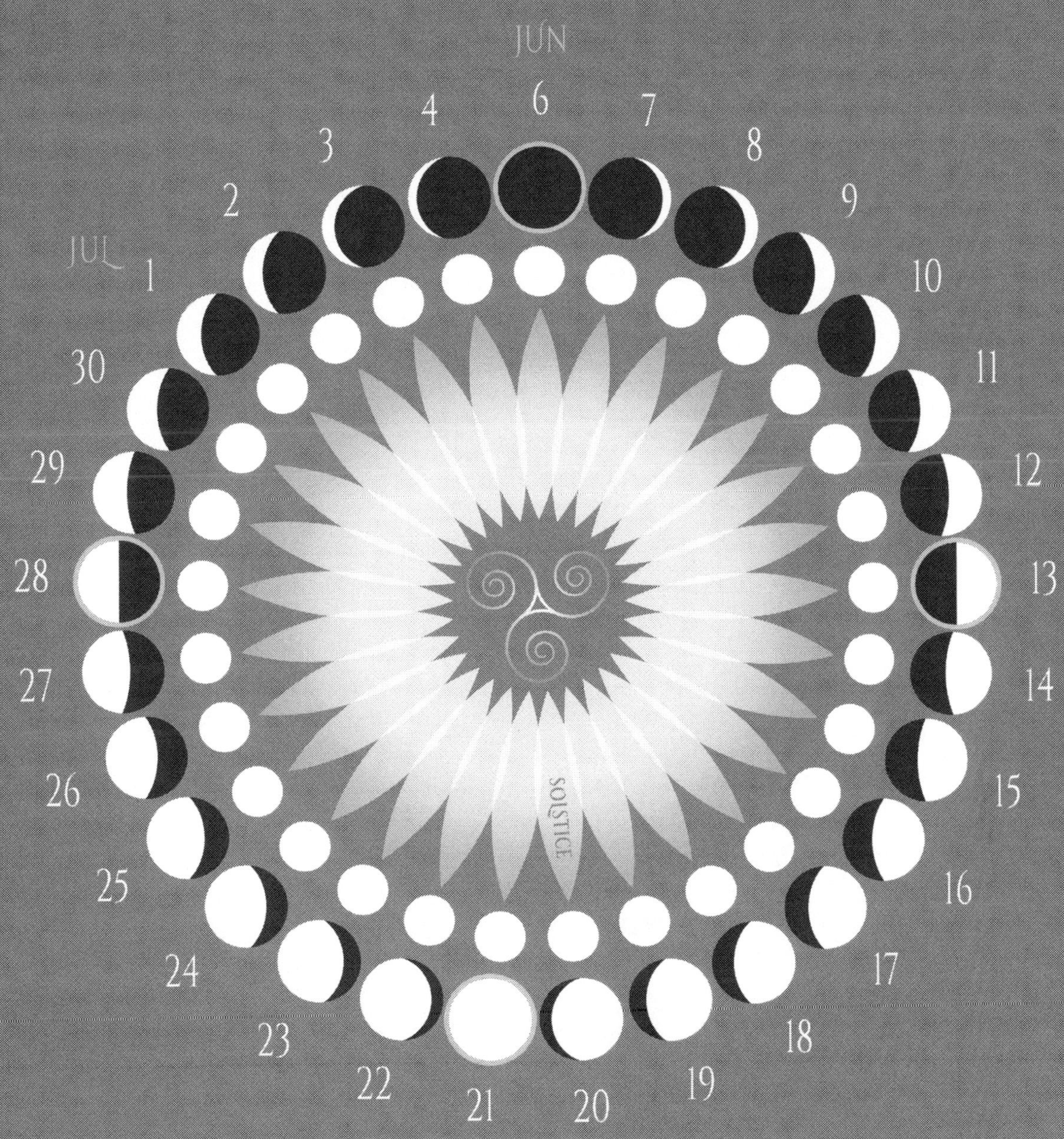

JUNE

SU	MO	TU	WE	TH	FR	SA
						1
2	3	4	5	6	7	8
9	10	11	12	13	14	15
16	17	18	19	20	21	22
23	24	25	26	27	28	29
30						

JULY

SU	MO	TU	WE	TH	FR	SA
	1	2	3	4	5	6
7	8	9	10	11	12	13
14	15	16	17	18	19	20
21	22	23	24	25	26	27
28	29	30	31			

SEATTLE 05:37 TH JUN 6 NEW MOON

intention

NEW YORK 08:37
TH JUN 6

LONDON 13:37
TH JUN 6

HONG KONG 20:37
TH JUN 6

FR JUN 7

SU JUN 9

MO JUN 10 

 TU JUN 11

WE JUN 12

TH JUN 13 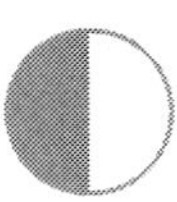

 FR JUN 14

SA JUN 15 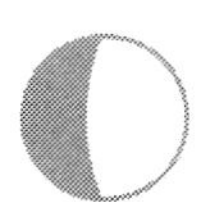

SU JUN 16 

MO JUN 17

TU JUN 18

WE JUN 19

TH JUN 20

13:50 SUMMER SOLSTICE

expression

SU JUN 23

MO JUN 24

WE JUN 26 

TH JUN 27

FR JUN 28

SA JUN 29 

 SU JUN 30

MO JUL 1

TU JUL 2

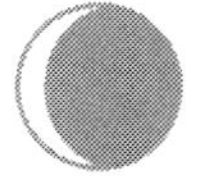

WE JUL 3

TH JUL 4

JULY 5 2024 TO AUGUST 3 2024

JUL

5 6 7 8 9 10 11 12 13 14 15 16 17 18 19 20 21 22 23 24 25 26 27 28 29 30 31

AUG

1 2 3

JULY

SU	MO	TU	WE	TH	FR	SA
	1	2	3	4	5	6
7	8	9	10	11	12	13
14	15	16	17	18	19	20
21	22	23	24	25	26	27
28	29	30	31			

AUGUST

SU	MO	TU	WE	TH	FR	SA
				1	2	3
4	5	6	7	8	9	10
11	12	13	14	15	16	17
18	19	20	21	22	23	24
25	26	27	28	29	30	31

SEATTLE 15:57 FR JUL 5  NEW MOON

intention

● NEW YORK 18:57 FR JUL 5 ● LONDON 23:57 FR JUL 5 ● HONG KONG 06:57 SA JUL 6

SA JUL 6 

SU JUL 7

MO JUL 8

TU JUL 9 

 WE JUL 10

TH JUL 11 

FR JUL 12

SA JUL 13

SU JUL 14

MO JUL 15 

TU JUL 16

WE JUL 17

TH JUL 18 

FR JUL 19

SA JUL 20

expression

MO JUL 22

TU JUL 23

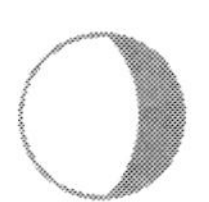

WE JUL 24

FR JUL 26 

SA JUL 27

SU JUL 28

MO JUL 29

TU JUL 30

WE JUL 31

TH AUG 1

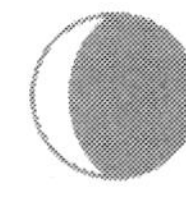

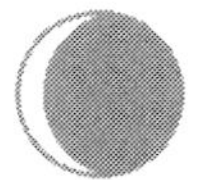

FR AUG 2

SA AUG 3

AUGUST 4 2024 TO SEPTEMBER 1 2024

SEP AUG

1 4 5 6 7 8 9 10 11 12 13 14 15 16 17 18 19 20 21 22 23 24 25 26 27 28 29 30 31

AUGUST

SU	MO	TU	WE	TH	FR	SA
				1	2	3
4	5	6	7	8	9	10
11	12	13	14	15	16	17
18	19	20	21	22	23	24
25	26	27	28	29	30	31

SEPTEMBER

SU	MO	TU	WE	TH	FR	SA
1	2	3	4	5	6	7
8	9	10	11	12	13	14
15	16	17	18	19	20	21
22	23	24	25	26	27	28
29	30					

SEATTLE 04:13 SU AUG 4 NEW MOON

intention

NEW YORK 07:13
SU AUG 4

LONDON 12:13
SU AUG 4

HONG KONG 19:13
SU AUG 4

MO AUG 5 

 TU AUG 6

WE AUG 7 

TH AUG 8

FR AUG 9

SA AUG 10

SU AUG 11

MO AUG 12

TU AUG 13

WE AUG 14

TH AUG 15

FR AUG 16

SA AUG 17

SU AUG 18

expression

WE AUG 21

TH AUG 22

SA AUG 24 

SU AUG 25

MO AUG 26

TU AUG 27 

WE AUG 28

FR AUG 30 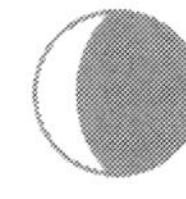

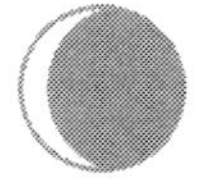 SA AUG 31

SU SEP 1

SEPTEMBER 2 2024 TO OCTOBER 1 2024

OCT SEP

2 3 4 5 6 7 8 9 10 11 12 13 14 15 16 17 18 19 20 21 22 23 24 25 26 27 28 29 30 1

EQUINOX

SEPTEMBER

SU	MO	TU	WE	TH	FR	SA
1	2	3	4	5	6	7
8	9	10	11	12	13	14
15	16	17	18	19	20	21
22	23	24	25	26	27	28
29	30					

OCTOBER

SU	MO	TU	WE	TH	FR	SA
		1	2	3	4	5
6	7	8	9	10	11	12
13	14	15	16	17	18	19
20	21	22	23	24	25	26
27	28	29	30	31		

SEATTLE 18:55 MO SEP 2 NEW MOON

intention

NEW YORK 21:55 MO SEP 2 • LONDON 02:55 TU SEP 3 • HONG KONG 09:55 TU SEP 3

TU SEP 3 

 WE SEP 4

TH SEP 5

FR SEP 6 

 SA SEP 7

SU SEP 8 

MO SEP 9 

 TU SEP 10

WE SEP 11 

TH SEP 12 

 FR SEP 13

SA SEP 14 

SU SEP 15 

MO SEP 16

SEATTLE 19:34 TU SEP 17  FULL MOON

expression

LUNAR ECLIPSE

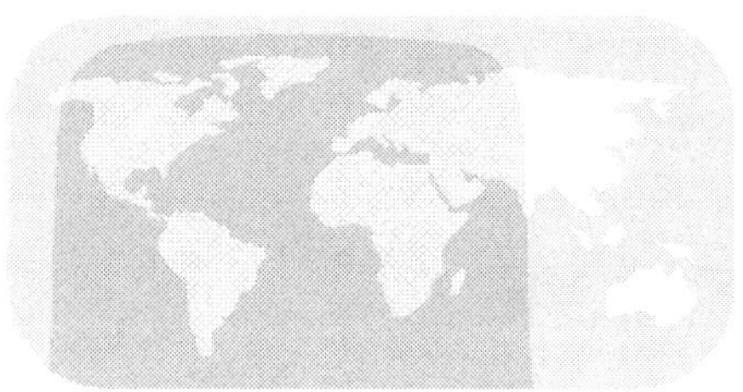

PARTIAL SEP 17-18

○ NEW YORK 22:34 ○ LONDON 03:34 ○ HONG KONG 10:34

TU SEP 17 WE SEP 18 WE SEP 18

WE SEP 18

TH SEP 19 

FR SEP 20

TU OCT 1

OCTOBER 2 2024 TO OCTOBER 31 2024

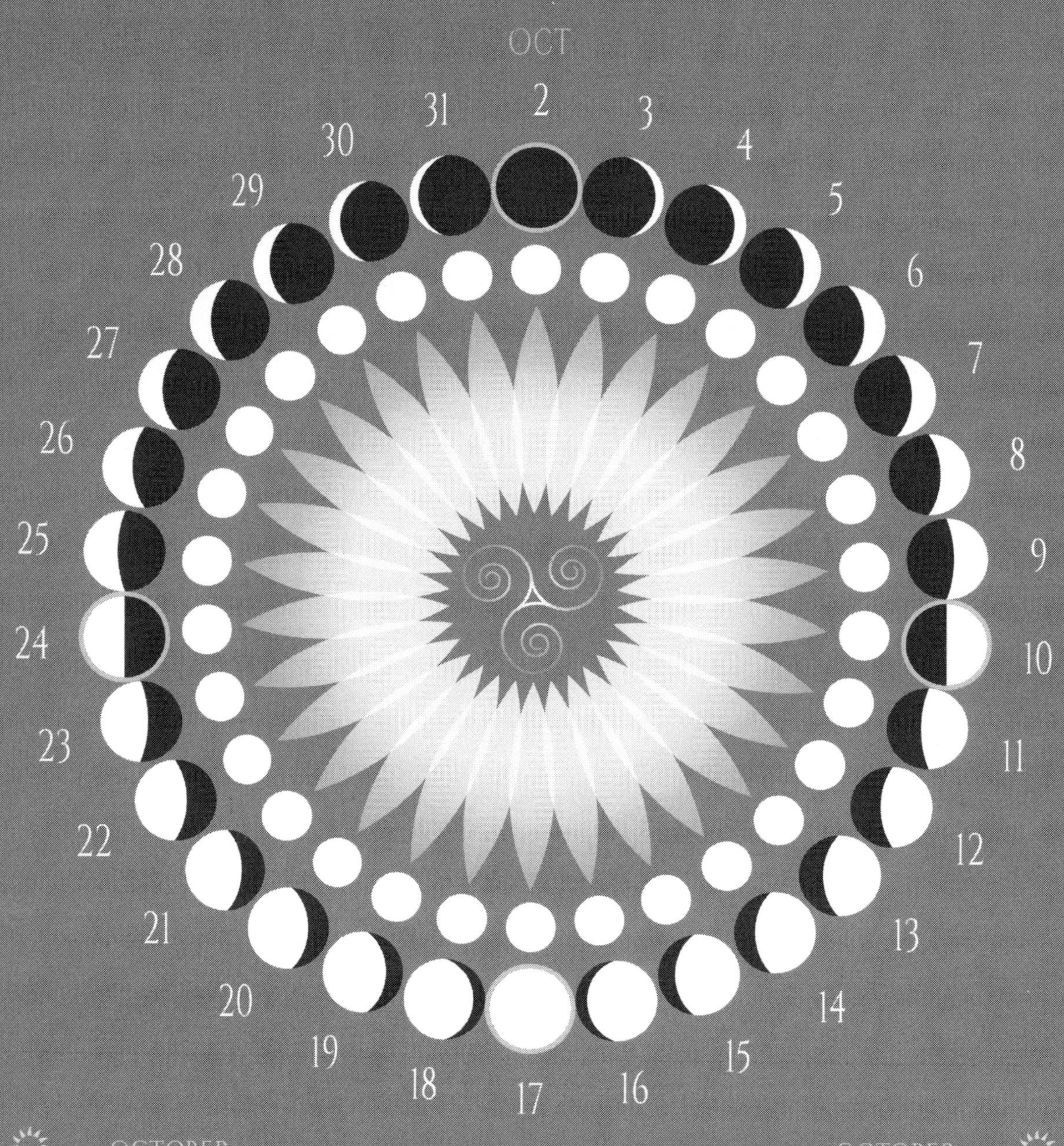

OCTOBER

SU	MO	TU	WE	TH	FR	SA
		1	2	3	4	5
6	7	8	9	10	11	12
13	14	15	16	17	18	19
20	21	22	23	24	25	26
27	28	29	30	31		

OCTOBER

SU	MO	TU	WE	TH	FR	SA
		1	2	3	4	5
6	7	8	9	10	11	12
13	14	15	16	17	18	19
20	21	22	23	24	25	26
27	28	29	30	31		

SEATTLE 11:49 WE OCT 2 NEW MOON

intention

SOLAR ECLIPSE

ANNULAR OCT 2

NEW YORK 14:49 WE OCT 2 · LONDON 19:49 WE OCT 2 · HONG KONG 02:49 TH OCT 3

TH OCT 3 

 FR OCT 4

SA OCT 5

SU OCT 6

MO OCT 7

TU OCT 8

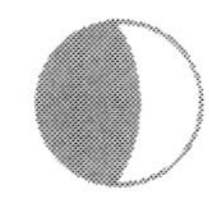

WE OCT 9 

TH OCT 10

FR OCT 11 

SA OCT 12

SU OCT 13

MO OCT 14 

TU OCT 15

WE OCT 16

expression

SA OCT 19

SU OCT 20

MO OCT 21

TU OCT 22 

 WE OCT 23

TH OCT 24

FR OCT 25 

SA OCT 26

SU OCT 27

MO OCT 28 

TU OCT 29

TH OCT 31 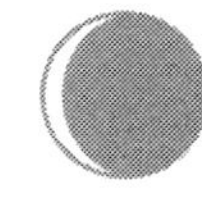

NOVEMBER 1 2024 TO NOVEMBER 29 2024

NOVEMBER

SU	MO	TU	WE	TH	FR	SA
					1	2
3	4	5	6	7	8	9
10	11	12	13	14	15	16
17	18	19	20	21	22	23
24	25	26	27	28	29	30

NOVEMBER

SU	MO	TU	WE	TH	FR	SA
					1	2
3	4	5	6	7	8	9
10	11	12	13	14	15	16
17	18	19	20	21	22	23
24	25	26	27	28	29	30

SEATTLE 05:47 FR NOV 1 NEW MOON

intention

NEW YORK 08:47
FR NOV 1

LONDON 12:47
FR NOV 1

HONG KONG 20:47
FR NOV 1

SA NOV 2 

TU NOV 5

WE NOV 6

TH NOV 7

FR NOV 8 

 SA NOV 9

MO NOV 11

WE NOV 13 

expression

SU NOV 17 

WE NOV 20 

 TH NOV 21

FR NOV 22

SA NOV 23 

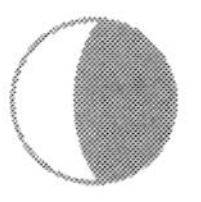

SU NOV 24

MO NOV 25

TU NOV 26

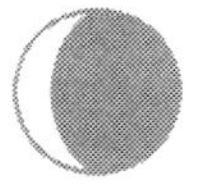

WE NOV 27

TH NOV 28

FR NOV 29

NOVEMBER 30 2024 TO DECEMBER 29 2024

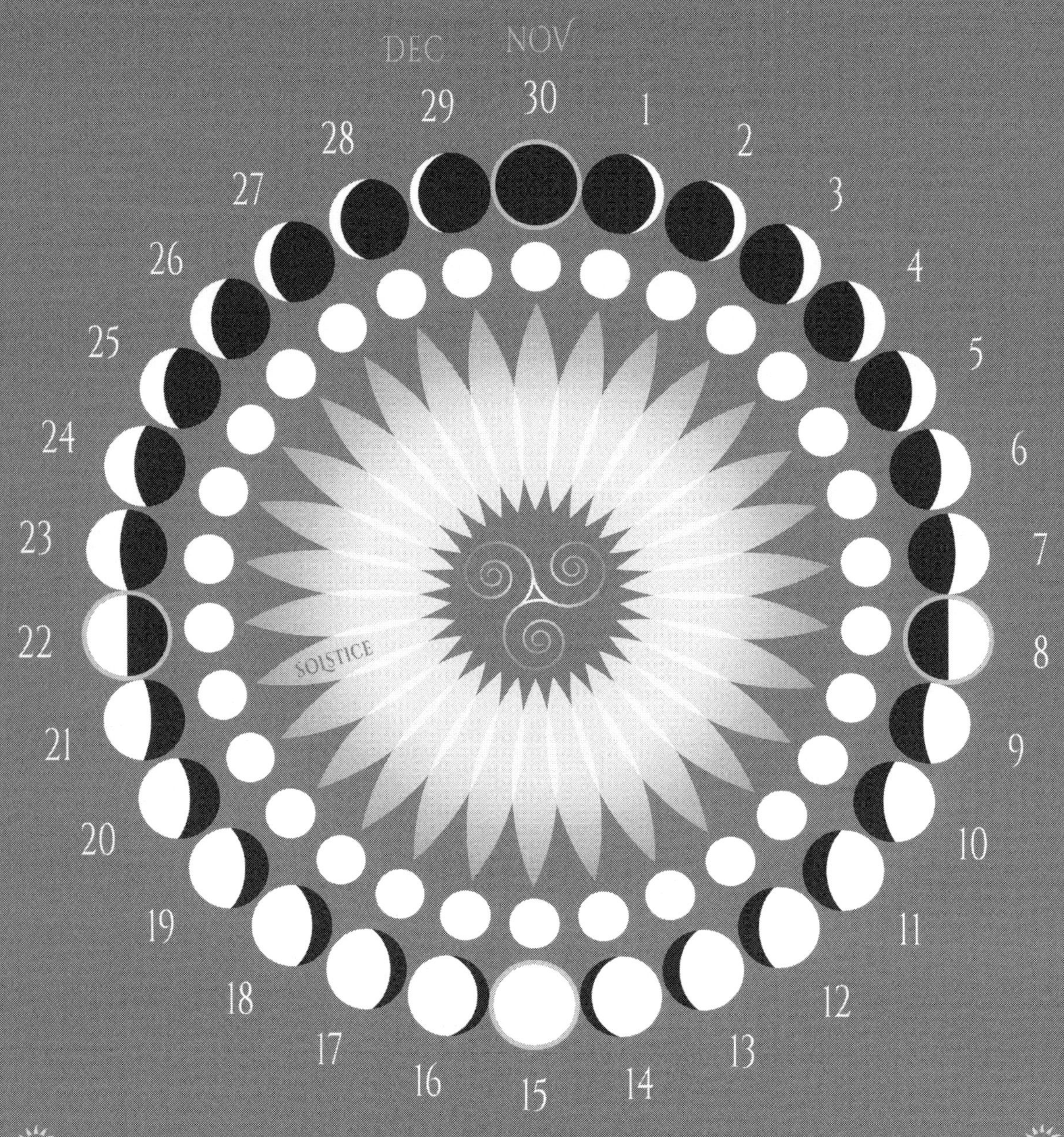

NOVEMBER

SU	MO	TU	WE	TH	FR	SA
					1	2
3	4	5	6	7	8	9
10	11	12	13	14	15	16
17	18	19	20	21	22	23
24	25	26	27	28	29	30

DECEMBER

SU	MO	TU	WE	TH	FR	SA
1	2	3	4	5	6	7
8	9	10	11	12	13	14
15	16	17	18	19	20	21
22	23	24	25	26	27	28
29	30	31				

SEATTLE 22:21 SA NOV 30 NEW MOON

intention

NEW YORK 01:21 SU DEC 1

LONDON 06:21 SU DEC 1

HONG KONG 14:21 SU DEC 1

SU DEC 1

MO DEC 2

TU DEC 3

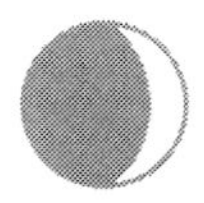

WE DEC 4 

 TH DEC 5

FR DEC 6

SA DEC 7 

 SU DEC 8

MO DEC 9

TU DEC 10 

 WE DEC 11

TH DEC 12 

FR DEC 13

SA DEC 14

expression

TU DEC 17

WE DEC 18

FR DEC 20 

SA DEC 21

01:20 WINTER SOLSTICE

SU DEC 22

MO DEC 23 

 TU DEC 24

WE DEC 25

TH DEC 26 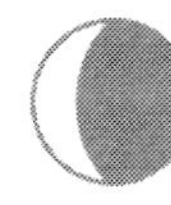

 FR DEC 27

SU DEC 29

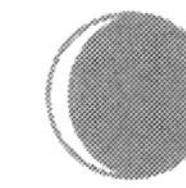

WINTER

INFANT / CRONE
BIRTH / DEATH

NOURISH

YIN OF YIN

AUTUMN

MAGA
MENOPAUSE

GATHER

YANG TO YIN

YIN TO YANG

GROW

MAIDEN
MENARCHE

SPRING

YANG OF YANG

MOVE

BIRTH / CREATION
MOTHER

SUMMER

SEATTLE 14:26 MO DEC 30 ● NEW MOON

intention

● NEW YORK 17:26 ● LONDON 22:26 ● HONG KONG 06:26

MO DEC 30 MO DEC 30 TU DEC 31

I am very proud to share that the entire production of this seventh edition has been led by womxn and womxn owned businesses.

The design of this diary was facilitated by www.99designs.com where I chose to work with Thora (www.99designs.com/profiles/thora) whose illustrations and graphic design work make this diary as beautiful as it is.

The printing and binding of this diary was facilitated by Girlie Press in Seattle, WA (www.girliepress.com)

If you would like to receive regular emails on each new and full moon offering moon inspired art and poetry, please join our mailing list via our website below

www.13moonsdiary.com